In Celebration of

_____

_____

Date

_____

Guest Name
(address/phone #/email)

Notes

_____

_____

_____

_____

_____

_____

_____

_____

_____

_____

_____

_____

_____

_____

Guest Name
(address/phone #/email)

Notes

_____

_____

_____

_____

Guest Name
(address/phone #/email)

Notes

_____

_____

_____

_____

_____

_____

_____

_____

_____

_____

_____

_____

_____

Guest Name
(address/phone #/email)

Notes

_____

_____

_____

_____

Guest Name
(address/phone #/email)

Notes

Guest Name
(address/phone #/email)

Notes

Guest Name
(address/phone #/email)

Notes

_____

_____

_____

_____

_____

_____

_____

_____

_____

_____

_____

_____

_____

_____

Guest Name
(address/phone #/email)

Notes

_____

_____

_____

_____

Guest Name
(address/phone #/email)

Notes

Guest Name
(address/phone #/email)

Notes

_____

_____

_____

_____

_____

_____

_____

_____

_____

_____

_____

_____

Guest Name
(address/phone #/email)

Notes

Guest Name
(address/phone #/email)

Notes

_____

_____

_____

_____

_____

_____

_____

_____

_____

_____

_____

_____

_____

_____

_____

Guest Name
(address/phone #/email)

Notes

_____

_____

_____

_____

_____

_____

_____

_____

_____

_____

_____

_____

_____

Guest Name
(address/phone #/email)

Notes

_____

_____

_____

_____

_____

_____

_____

_____

_____

_____

_____

Guest Name
(address/phone #/email)

Notes

Guest Name
(address/phone #/email)

Notes

Guest Name
(address/phone #/email)

Notes

_____

_____

_____

_____

Guest Name
(address/phone #/email)

Notes

_____

_____

_____

_____

_____

_____

_____

_____

_____

_____

_____

_____

_____

Guest Name
(address/phone #/email)

Notes

Guest Name
(address/phone #/email)

Notes

_____

_____

_____

_____

Guest Name
(address/phone #/email)

Notes

_____

_____

_____

_____

Guest Name
(address/phone #/email)

Notes

_____

_____

_____

_____

Guest Name
(address/phone #/email)

Notes

_____

_____

_____

_____

_____

_____

_____

_____

_____

_____

_____

_____

_____

_____

Guest Name
(address/phone #/email)

Notes

_____

_____

_____

_____

Guest Name
(address/phone #/email)

Notes

_____

_____

_____

_____

_____

_____

_____

_____

_____

_____

_____

_____

Guest Name
(address/phone #/email)

Notes

_____

_____

_____

_____

_____

_____

_____

_____

_____

_____

_____

_____

Guest Name
(address/phone #/email)

Notes

_____

_____

_____

_____

_____

_____

_____

_____

_____

_____

_____

_____

_____

_____

Guest Name
(address/phone #/email)

Notes

_____

_____

_____

_____

_____

_____

_____

_____

_____

_____

_____

_____

_____

Guest Name
(address/phone #/email)

Notes

_____

_____

_____

_____

_____

_____

_____

_____

_____

_____

_____

_____

_____

Guest Name
(address/phone #/email)

Notes

_____

_____

_____

_____

Guest Name
(address/phone #/email)

Notes

_____

_____

_____

_____

_____

_____

_____

_____

_____

_____

_____

_____

_____

Guest Name
(address/phone #/email)

Notes

_____

_____

_____

_____

Guest Name
(address/phone #/email)

Notes

Guest Name
(address/phone #/email)

Notes

_____

_____

_____

_____

_____

_____

_____

_____

_____

_____

_____

_____

Guest Name
(address/phone #/email)

Notes

_____

_____

_____

_____

Guest Name
(address/phone #/email)

_____

_____

_____

_____

Notes

_____

_____

_____

_____

_____

_____

_____

_____

_____

_____

_____

Guest Name
(address/phone #/email)

Notes

_____

_____

_____

_____

Guest Name
(address/phone #/email)

Notes

_____

_____

_____

_____

_____

_____

_____

_____

_____

_____

_____

_____

_____

_____

Guest Name
(address/phone #/email)

Notes

Guest Name
(address/phone #/email)

Notes

Guest Name
(address/phone #/email)

Notes

_____

_____

_____

_____

_____

_____

_____

_____

_____

_____

_____

_____

_____

Guest Name
(address/phone #/email)

Notes

_____

_____

_____

_____

Guest Name
(address/phone #/email)

Notes

_____

_____

_____

_____

_____

_____

_____

_____

_____

_____

_____

_____

_____

_____

Guest Name
(address/phone #/email)

Notes

_____

_____

_____

_____

_____

_____

_____

_____

_____

_____

_____

_____

_____

Guest Name
(address/phone #/email)

Notes

_____

_____

_____

_____

_____

_____

_____

_____

_____

_____

_____

_____

_____

_____

_____

Guest Name
(address/phone #/email)

Notes

_____

_____

_____

_____

Guest Name
(address/phone #/email)

Notes

_____

_____

_____

_____

_____

_____

_____

_____

_____

_____

_____

_____

_____

Guest Name
(address/phone #/email)

Notes

Guest Name
(address/phone #/email)

Notes

_____

_____

_____

_____

_____

_____

_____

_____

_____

_____

_____

_____

_____

_____

Guest Name
(address/phone #/email)

Notes

_____

_____

_____

_____

_____

_____

_____

_____

_____

_____

_____

_____

_____

Guest Name
(address/phone #/email)

Notes

_____

_____

_____

_____

_____

_____

_____

_____

_____

_____

_____

_____

_____

Guest Name
(address/phone #/email)

Notes

_____

_____

_____

_____

_____

_____

_____

_____

_____

_____

_____

_____

_____

_____

Guest Name
(address/phone #/email)

Notes

_____

_____

_____

_____

Guest Name
(address/phone #/email)

Notes

_____

_____

_____

_____

_____

_____

_____

_____

_____

_____

_____

_____

Guest Name
(address/phone #/email)

Notes

_____

_____

_____

_____

Guest Name
(address/phone #/email)

Notes

_____

_____

_____

_____

_____

_____

_____

_____

_____

_____

_____

_____

_____

Guest Name
(address/phone #/email)

Notes

Guest Name
(address/phone #/email)

Notes

_____

_____

_____

_____

Guest Name
(address/phone #/email)

Notes

_____

_____

_____

_____

_____

_____

_____

_____

_____

_____

_____

_____

_____

Guest Name
(address/phone #/email)

Notes

_____

_____

_____

_____

_____

_____

_____

_____

_____

_____

_____

_____

Guest Name
(address/phone #/email)

Notes

Guest Name
(address/phone #/email)

Notes

_____

_____

_____

_____

_____

_____

_____

_____

_____

_____

_____

_____

Guest Name
(address/phone #/email)

Notes

_____

_____

_____

_____

_____

_____

_____

_____

_____

_____

_____

_____

_____

Guest Name
(address/phone #/email)

Notes

Guest Name
(address/phone #/email)

Notes

Guest Name
(address/phone #/email)

Notes

_____

_____

_____

_____

_____

_____

_____

_____

_____

_____

_____

_____

_____

_____

Guest Name
(address/phone #/email)

Notes

_____

_____

_____

_____

_____

_____

_____

_____

_____

_____

_____

_____

_____

_____

Guest Name
(address/phone #/email)

Notes

_____

_____

_____

_____

_____

_____

_____

_____

_____

_____

_____

_____

_____

Guest Name
(address/phone #/email)

Notes

Guest Name
(address/phone #/email)

Notes

Guest Name
(address/phone #/email)

Notes

_____

_____

_____

_____

_____

_____

_____

_____

_____

_____

_____

_____

_____

_____

Guest Name
(address/phone #/email)

Notes

_____

_____

_____

_____

_____

_____

_____

_____

_____

_____

_____

_____

_____

Guest Name
(address/phone #/email)

Notes

Guest Name
(address/phone #/email)

Notes

_____

_____

_____

_____

_____

_____

_____

_____

_____

_____

_____

_____

_____

_____

Guest Name
(address/phone #/email)

Notes

_____

_____

_____

_____

_____

_____

_____

_____

_____

_____

_____

_____

_____

Guest Name
(address/phone #/email)

Notes

_____

_____

_____

_____

_____

_____

_____

_____

_____

_____

_____

_____

_____

Guest Name
(address/phone #/email)

Notes

_____

_____

_____

_____

_____

_____

_____

_____

_____

_____

_____

_____

_____

Guest Name
(address/phone #/email)

Notes

Guest Name
(address/phone #/email)

Notes

Guest Name
(address/phone #/email)

Notes

_____

_____

_____

_____

_____

_____

_____

_____

_____

_____

_____

_____

_____

_____

_____

Guest Name
(address/phone #/email)

Notes

_____

_____

_____

_____

_____

_____

_____

_____

_____

_____

_____

_____

_____

_____

Guest Name
(address/phone #/email)

Notes

_____

_____

_____

_____

_____

_____

_____

_____

_____

_____

_____

_____

_____

Guest Name
(address/phone #/email)

Notes

_____

_____

_____

_____

_____

_____

_____

_____

_____

_____

_____

_____

_____

Guest Name
(address/phone #/email)

_____

_____

_____

_____

Notes

_____

_____

_____

_____

_____

_____

_____

_____

_____

_____

_____

Guest Name
(address/phone #/email)

Notes

_____

_____

_____

_____

_____

_____

_____

_____

_____

_____

_____

_____

_____

_____

_____

_____

Guest Name
(address/phone #/email)

Notes

_____

_____

_____

_____

_____

_____

_____

_____

_____

_____

_____

_____

_____

_____

_____

Guest Name
(address/phone #/email)

 **Notes**

_____

_____

_____

_____

_____

_____

_____

_____

_____

_____

_____

_____

_____

_____

Guest Name
(address/phone #/email)

Notes

_____

_____

_____

_____

_____

_____

_____

_____

_____

_____

_____

_____

_____

Guest Name
(address/phone #/email)

Notes

_____

_____

_____

_____

Guest Name
(address/phone #/email)

Notes

Guest Name
(address/phone #/email)

Notes

_____

_____

_____

_____

_____

_____

_____

_____

_____

_____

_____

_____

_____

Guest Name
(address/phone #/email)

Notes

_____

_____

_____

_____

_____

_____

_____

_____

_____

_____

_____

_____

_____

Guest Name
(address/phone #/email)

Notes

_____

_____

_____

_____

_____

_____

_____

_____

_____

_____

_____

Guest Name
(address/phone #/email)

Notes

_____

_____

_____

_____

_____

_____

_____

_____

_____

_____

_____

_____

_____

Guest Name
(address/phone #/email)

Notes

Guest Name
(address/phone #/email)

Notes

_____

_____

_____

_____

Guest Name
(address/phone #/email)

Notes

Guest Name
(address/phone #/email)

Notes

Guest Name
(address/phone #/email)

Notes

Guest Name
(address/phone #/email)

Notes

_____

_____

_____

_____

_____

_____

_____

_____

_____

_____

_____

_____

_____

Guest Name
(address/phone #/email)

Notes

_____

_____

_____

_____

_____

_____

_____

_____

_____

_____

_____

_____

_____

Guest Name
(address/phone #/email)

Notes

_____

_____

_____

_____

_____

_____

_____

_____

_____

_____

_____

Guest Name
(address/phone #/email)

Notes

_____

_____

_____

_____

_____

_____

_____

_____

_____

_____

_____

_____

_____

_____

Guest Name
(address/phone #/email)

Notes

Guest Name
(address/phone #/email)

Notes

_____

_____

_____

_____

_____

_____

_____

_____

_____

_____

_____

_____

Guest Name
(address/phone #/email)

Notes

_____

_____

_____

_____

_____

_____

_____

_____

_____

_____

_____

_____

_____

_____

Guest Name
(address/phone #/email)

Notes

Guest Name
(address/phone #/email)

Notes

Guest Name
(address/phone #/email)

Notes

_____

_____

_____

_____

Guest Name
(address/phone #/email)

Notes

Guest Name
(address/phone #/email)

Notes

Made in United States
Orlando, FL
08 September 2022